MW01275221

Especially for

Pastor Janice Juss

From

The Shaw Family

Date

Oct. 16, 2011

# Simple
# Pleasures

*A Celebration of Life's Simple Pleasures*

BARBOUR
PUBLISHING

Published by Barbour Publishing, Inc., P.O. Box 719, Uhrichsville, Ohio 44683, www.barbourbooks.com

*Our mission is to publish and distribute inspirational products offering exceptional value and biblical encouragement to the masses.*

 Member of the
Evangelical Christian
Publishers Association

Printed in China.

# Contents

# Celebrate Life's
# Simple Pleasures

*Enjoy the little things, for one day you may
look back and discover they were the big things.*
UNKNOWN

Think about all the lovely things God has given for your
enjoyment—not just "stuff" but the so-called "little things" in
life that really matter. Spending time with family and friends,
warm sunshine on a spring day, your daily conversations with
God. . . The fact is, the Master Creator has blessed you with
so many simple pleasures, that you could have an "I've been
blessed" celebration every day of the week. Read on. . .and
thank Him for the many blessings He's placed in your life!

Blessings

*"I thank You and praise You, O God of my fathers; You have given me wisdom and might."*

DANIEL 2:23 NKJV

# A Little Time with God

Susan headed out of her house in the same way she always did—in a hurry, guiding two children before her, double-checking their backpacks as she went and reminding them of chores and practices scheduled for that afternoon. "Remember, 3:30 is ballet; 4:00 is soccer. I'll pick you up after school, but I have to go back to work, so—"

She stopped as her coat snagged on a bush. "What?—" She looked down to find her hem caught firmly by a cluster of thorns. As she stooped to untangle the cloth, the stem bent suddenly, and Susan found herself nose-to-petal with a rose. It smelled glorious, and she paused, laughing.

When Susan had planted the bush, a friend had asked why. "You never stop long enough to enjoy even what God drops in front of you. What makes you think you'll care about a rose?"

Susan glanced up toward the sky. "Thanks for grabbing me. I guess I should spend a little more time with You."

God blesses us every day in both great and simple ways. Children, friends, work, faith—all these things form a bountiful buffet of gifts, and caring for them isn't always enough. We need to spend a little time with the One who has granted us the blessings.

RAMONA RICHARDS

Every experience God gives us,
every person He puts into our lives,
is the perfect preparation for the
future that only He can see.

CORRIE TEN BOOM

# Guaranteed Blessing

*Your* Word says that You actually guarantee a blessing on everything I do! That's a promise I can count on, and one I revel in. It gives me the confidence that You will be with me in all that I do, blessing me at each and every turn. What an awesome promise! I arise today, assured of Your assistance, guidance, and approval of every good thing. There are no words to express how You make me feel. I am humbled in Your presence and renewed in Your light. I praise You, Lord!

Donna K. Maltese

*Just as you received Christ Jesus as Lord,*
*continue to live in him. . .strengthened in the*
*faith as you were taught, and overflowing*
*with thankfulness.*

COLOSSIANS 2:6–7 NIV

# Overflowing with Thanksgiving

When Annie was in college, she assumed she'd graduate with honors and land the job of her dreams. But in spite of her impressive transcript, the perfect job never materialized. An obscure major, a lack of experience, and a struggling economy meant Annie was lucky to get a job making a modest hourly wage, barely enough to pay the rent—definitely not enough for the little red sports car she'd had her eye on.

After a few months of working hard for little income, Annie was discouraged. In fact, she was becoming downright depressed. A chance encounter with an old family friend changed everything. This elderly woman had outlived two husbands and was now alone. Social security provided little income, but the woman didn't seem to mind. When asked how she managed, the dear woman's response was simple. "I don't have much," she said, "but life's a lot better when you focus on what you do have instead of what you don't."

In our affluent society it is easy to get caught up in the things we don't have or things we wish we had. However, a simple change in perspective can open our eyes to the many ways God has blessed us. Take a moment to make a list of your blessings. Soon you'll be overflowing with thanks!

JOANNA BLOSS

Above all else, know this:
Be prepared at all times for the
gifts of God and be ready always
for new ones. For God is a
thousand times more ready to give
than we are to receive.

MEISTER ECKHART

# Daily Benefits

*I* am loaded with benefits! Blessed beyond compare!
You, the God of my salvation, the Friend who laid down
His life for me, the One who is with me in fire, flood,
and famine, the One who will never leave me nor forsake me!
Today is a new day, and You have benefits waiting out there for
me. I begin the day in my walk toward You, leaving my burdens
behind and focusing on the benefits ahead. And when I come
to You at the close of the day, You will be waiting for me,
at the end of the path, with a good word.

DONNA K. MALTESE

*Blessed be the Lord,*
*who daily loads us with benefits,*
*the God of our salvation!*

PSALM 68:19 NKJV

Family

*For I will pour water upon him that is*
*thirsty, and floods upon the dry ground:*
*I will pour my spirit upon thy seed,*
*and my blessing upon thine offspring.*

Isaiah 44:3 kjv

# Poured Out Blessings

What is more refreshing than a cold glass of water after vigorous exercise or hard work? What a pleasure it is to enjoy this natural beverage. Yet how often do we see that simple glass of water as a blessing from God? What about the cool grass beneath our feet or the shade tree under which we relax? When we teach our children to say *bird* or *bunny*, do we acknowledge those creatures as delightful gifts from God?

God's blessings surround us. At times we realize they are there, but many of them are overlooked as common, everyday parts of life. We wonder why God isn't at work or doing more for us when in reality He is busy right before our eyes. We're just too distracted to notice. God is with His children. He meets our family's needs daily, and His gifts are wonderful. Let's teach our children to recognize and praise God's goodness. Perhaps as we do this, the scales will be lifted from our own eyes, and we will begin to see God's bounty for what it really is.

RACHEL QUILLIN

The happiest moments of my life have been the few which I have passed at home in the bosom of my family.

THOMAS JEFFERSON

# Unconditional Love

*L*ord, I thank You for my family members and those who are like family to me. I am grateful for their love and understanding. May I be loving in return—not only with those who love me, but even with those who are hard to be around. Your ways are merciful and kind, forgiving and good. Help me to reflect Your love, finding joy in loving others as You love me.

JACKIE M. JOHNSON

Let me live forever in your sanctuary,
safe beneath the shelter of your wings!
For you have heard my vows, O God.
You have given me an inheritance
reserved for those who fear your name.

PSALM 61:4–5 NLT

# A Family Name

Names have meaning. When a mother considers names for her expected baby, careful thought usually goes into the process. We use names to get someone's attention, but we also use them to show family ties. Our names do not define who we are; but for good or for bad, they do tell who we came from.

In times past, last names held even greater meaning because they linked distant relatives together. Often, people were referred to by their first name but also by their father's name, such as so-and-so, the son of so-and-so. This was certainly true in Shakespeare's tragedy, *Romeo and Juliet*. The Bible also records ancestral and descendant names. Christ was known as Jesus, the son of Joseph. In fact, the book of Matthew even records Christ's ancestral history dating back hundreds of years.

Some people are not proud of their last names. They might be linked back to ungodly people and events or may even be spelled or pronounced oddly. Fortunately, those who are believers enter into God's family and are given new names—the sons and daughters of the Most High God. Put that on your résumé!

KATE E. SCHMELZER

The family is one of nature's masterpieces.

GEORGE SANTAYANA

# When I Don't Know
# What to Pray

*Lord*, I don't always know what to pray for my extended family. But You know each of them—their hopes and dreams, needs and desires. I ask You to intercede with the power of Your Holy Spirit. May His deep groans translate into the words I can't express. Thank You, Lord, for filling in the gaps in my knowledge and ability. You are the God who knows all!

JACKIE M. JOHNSON

*Live in harmony with one another.*

ROMANS 12:16 NIV

# Friendship

*Cheerfully share your home
with those who need a meal
or a place to stay.*

1 PETER 4:9 NLT

# Hospitality and Friendship

When Anne was young, having company meant frenetically cleaning the house from floor to ceiling, shopping for groceries, and cooking elaborate meals. Company meant trying to make a good impression. As Anne anticipated company, her heart raced and she focused all her energy to make things perfect.

After several years of anxious entertaining, Anne heard her mentor describe how she did not worry what the house looked like when company came over. All that mattered to Anne's mentor was that when people were invited into her home, they would come as they were and she would receive them as she was. Anne's mentor put up no pretenses, cast aside anxiety related to "making impressions," and focused solely on *ministering* to her guests, as opposed to *impressing* her guests.

Shortly after this discussion, Anne had ten women coming to her home for the day, and she barely had time to cook or shop. Instead of panicking, Anne kept things simple. She left the floors as they were and simply cleaned the bathrooms and kitchen where cleaning really counted. Instead of planning elaborate meals, she prepared a simple breakfast—bagels, cream cheese, string cheese, fruit, orange juice, and coffee. Delicious. And instead of cooking lunch, she had a simple, hearty meal delivered by a local restaurant. Everyone enjoyed it. The day could not have gone better, and Anne relaxed and enjoyed the day as well.

JUNE HETZEL

*If you can eat today, enjoy the sunlight today, mix good cheer with friends today, enjoy it and bless God for it.*

HENRY WARD BEECHER

# Blessed with Friends

There are many wonderful things in this life, Lord. The smell of a baby's breath, the touch of a warm hand, the taste of dark chocolate—but a good word, deed, or thought from a friend is even better. There are times when I am so down. And then a friend blesses me and I think of You. It's because of You and the love that You give that makes us want to reach out to others. Thank You for blessing my life with friends.

DONNA K. MALTESE

*Two are better than one. . . .*
*If one falls down, his friend can help him up.*

ECCLESIASTES 4:9–10 NIV

# Here You Are!

*Jodie* lived in a predominantly Muslim country where she became a student of Arabic. She was invited to teach English to women in a mosque basement kindergarten classroom. For five months she met regularly with these women—Jodie wrestling with Arabic and those dozen women doing their best to learn English. They had only met a few times when the women's questions took on an added dimension of challenge for Jodie: They wanted to know about Christians and Christianity.

Do foreigners pray? Are Christians like the ones we see in movies from America? Do you believe that *Isa* is the Son of God?

Jodie struggled to answer their questions in her own weak Arabic. But she did the best she could, trusting God to use her in exposing these women to the truth of Jesus Christ. An unexpected blessing came from one of the young women in her group.

"I have prayed all my life that God would give me a Christian friend so I could understand her better," she said. "And here you are!"

Sometimes we pick our friends; sometimes our friends pick us. We may be years into a friendship and not recall how it started. But how wonderful to have a good friend! Maybe today is the day to tell someone, "I'm so glad you're my friend." Those few words may make her day.

KATHERINE DOUGLAS

The best things in life are never rationed. Friendship, loyalty, love do not require coupons.

George T. Hewitt

# Thank You for My Friendships

*Lord*, I thank You for my wonderful friends! As I think about the treasure chest of my close friends, casual friends, and acquaintances, I am grateful for the blessings and the joys each one brings to my life. Thank You for my "heart" friends, my loyal sister friends who listen, care, and encourage me. They are my faithful companions. I acknowledge that You, Lord, are the giver of all good gifts, and I thank You for Your provision in my friendships.

JACKIE M. JOHNSON

*A friend loveth at all times.*

PROVERBS 17:17 KJV

God's
Creation

*God's glory is on tour in the skies,*
*God-craft on exhibit across the horizon.*

PSALM 19:1 MSG

# The Grandeur of Creation

Look outside right now; better yet, go outside. Daytime or nighttime, it doesn't matter. Just look around you. If you live in a concrete jungle, look up at the sky. Imagine for a moment the immensity of God's creation, the grandeur of it. And yet, He calls mankind His most splendid creation—all the rest was called into being only to benefit His human creation. God values you above all else. Look up at the sky and consider that.

Rebecca Currington

Some people, in order to
discover God, read books.
But there is a great book:
the very appearance of created
things. Look above you!
Look below you!
Read it.

St. Augustine

# Wisdom of Creation

*God,* Your creation is so awesome. Everywhere I look, I see
Your handiwork. You have made it all. You have made me.
Continue to mold me and shape me into the person You want me
to be. Give me knowledge and wisdom in how best to serve You.

DONNA K. MALTESE

*{Jesus said}*, "Walk out into the
fields and look at the wildflowers."

MATTHEW 6:28 MSG

# The Details

*Our* God cares about details. You see it throughout His creation. Every species unique and every creature unique within its species. Human beings, created in His image and yet each one of a kind. Flowers and trees awash with color and refinement, even those growing along the highway, sown as it were by the wind. When you wonder if God is interested in the details of your life, consider the evidence demonstrated in nature. He cares about everything—no matter how inconsequential.

Rebecca Currington

God writes the gospel not in the
Bible alone, but on trees and
flowers and clouds and stars.

Martin Luther

# Asked to Be Cocreators

Lord, You formed all things. And afterward, You invited man to be your cocreator, allowing him to name things, do things, and serve You. Show me now, Lord, how You want me to employ my talents, my gifts, and myself to make this world a better place. Come to me now, Lord. Imprint upon my mind what You want me to do, which door You want me to walk through.

DONNA K. MALTESE

*And out of the ground the LORD God formed
every beast of the field, and every fowl of the air;
and brought them unto Adam to see what he would
call them: and whatsoever Adam called every living
creature, that was the name thereof.*

GENESIS 2:19 KJV

Joy

*A happy heart makes the face cheerful.*

PROVERBS 15:13 NIV

# The Secret of Serendipity

*Can* you remember the last time you laughed in wild abandon? Better yet, when was the last time you did something fun, outrageous, or out of the ordinary? Perhaps it is an activity you haven't done since you were a child, like slip down a waterslide, strap on a pair of ice skates, or pitch a tent and camp overnight.

Women often become trapped in the cycle of routine, and soon we lose our spontaneity. Children, on the other hand, are innately spontaneous. Giggling, they splash barefoot in rain puddles. Wide-eyed, they watch a kite soar toward the treetops. They make silly faces without inhibition; they see animal shapes in rock formations. In essence, they possess the secret of serendipity.

A happy heart turns life's situations into opportunities for fun. For instance, if a storm snuffs out the electricity, light a candle and play games, tell stories, or just enjoy the quiet. When we seek innocent pleasures, we glean the benefits of a happy heart.

Jesus said, "I am come that they might have life, and that they might have it more abundantly" (John 10:10 KJV). God wants us to enjoy life, and when we do, it lightens our load and changes our countenance.

So try a bit of whimsy just for fun. And rediscover the secret of serendipity.

TINA KRAUSE

51

Half the joy of life is in little things
taken on the run. Let us run if we
must—even the sands do that—but
let us keep our hearts young and
our eyes open that nothing worth
our while shall escape us.
And everything is worth its while if
we only grasp it and its significance.

C. VICTOR CHERBULIEZ

# The Joy of Knowing Jesus

*Jesus*, knowing You brings me joy! I am so glad that I am saved and on my way to heaven. Thank You for the abundant life You provide. I can smile because I know that You love me. I can be positive because You have the power to heal, restore, and revive. Your presence brings me joy—just being with You is such a privilege. You are awesome, and I delight to know I can tell others about You.

JACKIE M. JOHNSON

*Satisfy us in the morning with your unfailing love, that we may sing for joy and be glad all our days.*

PSALM 90:14 NIV

# A Life of Joy

*Webster's* dictionary defines joy as "emotion evoked by well-being, success, or good fortune." When was the last time you experienced joy? Was it last month? Last week? Today?

There are many joyful occasions: a birthday, an anniversary, a job promotion, a wedding, the birth of a baby. . .the list can go on. But do we need a big event to give us joy? Many ordinary moments can bring joy as well: getting a close parking spot at the mall, finding a ten-dollar bill in your pocket. . .again, the list continues.

First Thessalonians 5:16 (NLT) tells us to "always be joyful." That doesn't mean we need to take pleasure when things go wrong in life, smiling all the while. Rather, God wants us to maintain a spirit of joy, knowing that He has provided happy times and will carry us through the hard times.

Ever notice how a joyful spirit is contagious? When you're around someone who is full of joy, it's easy to find yourself sharing in that joy. Maybe you could be that person today, bringing smiles to others. When you find delight in the ordinary moments, they will catch the joy.

JENNIFER HAHN

{God} knows everything about us.
And He cares about everything.
Moreover, He can manage every
situation. And He loves us!
Surely this is enough to open the
wellsprings of joy. . . . And joy is
always a source of strength.

HANNAH WHITALL SMITH

# Finding Joy in God's Presence

*Lord*, draw me closer to You. In Your presence is fullness of joy—and I want to be filled. Knowing I am loved by You makes me glad; I cannot imagine life without You. With You there is light; without You, darkness. With You there is pleasure; without You, pain. You care, You comfort; You really listen. Here, in Your presence, I am loved, I am renewed, and I am very happy.

JACKIE M. JOHNSON

*Always be joyful. Never stop praying.*
*Be thankful in all circumstances, for this is*
*God's will for you who belong to Christ Jesus.*

1 Thessalonians 5:16–18 NLT

# Loving
# Others

*For we have great joy and consolation in your love, because the hearts of the saints have been refreshed by you, brother.*

PHILEMON 1:7 NKJV

# Refreshing Gift

*Unsure* whether she could continue in the race, the woman looked ahead. A small stand wasn't far down the road. She could see the line of cups at the edge of the table—drinks set out to refresh the runners. The sight encouraged her enough to give her the needed confidence to finish the race.

Encouragement is a wonderful gift. Simple gestures mean so much to those around us. We don't have to make big, splashy scenes to give someone a boost. Our smile can lift someone who is discouraged. A sincere thank-you or a quick hug conveys a wealth of love, gratitude, and appreciation. We all have the opportunity to make small overtures to those around us.

Jesus always took the time for those who reached out to Him. In a crowd of people, He stopped to help a woman who touched Him. His quiet love extended to everyone who asked, whether verbally or with unspoken need.

God brings people into our path who need our encouragement. We must consider those around us. Smile and thank the waitress, the cashier, the people who help in small ways. Cheering others can have the effect of an energizing drink of water so that they will be able to finish the race with a smile.

NANCY FARRIER

The love we give away
is the only love we keep.

ELBERT HUBBARD

# Helping Each Other

Lord, my gift not only serves You but helps others as well. What a blessing! Be with me as I sacrifice my time and energy today to minister to others. This is my calling. This is my gift. And I do it all in Your love.

DONNA K. MALTESE

"Give, and it will be given to you.
A good measure, pressed down, shaken
together and running over, will be poured
into your lap. For with the measure you use,
it will be measured to you."

LUKE 6:38 NIV

# More Blessed to Give

*When* Cassie learned that her church's homeless ministry needed help, she volunteered, eager to give what she could. Lending a hand seemed like the right thing to do, and she expected to find lots of needy people with whom she could share her gifts. She found plenty of needy people, and she definitely lent a hand. However, what she hadn't expected was to be blessed so much. Not only did she make some new friends, but they taught her a great deal about thankfulness, contentment, and how to make the best of a hard situation.

In God's economy, giving means receiving. When we give to others, we receive more than the satisfaction of a job well done. Jesus promises blessing when we give to others. They can be simple blessings, such as a smile or a kind word of thanks. Blessings can also be life changing, such as making a new friend or acquiring a new skill. Getting something shouldn't be our motivation for serving others, but it is an added bonus. What can you do today to be a blessing to others?

JOANNA BLOSS

What does love look like? It has the hands to help others. It has the feet to hasten to the poor and needy. It has eyes to see misery and want. It has the ears to hear the sighs and sorrows of men. That is what love looks like.

St. Augustine

# A Heart to Serve

*Lord*, I pray for a spirit of compassion. Help me to care about the needs of others and have genuine love for the ones I serve. Pour into me Your caring, kind spirit, so I can be a blessing and minister out of a full heart. Fill me to overflowing so my ministry will be effective, growing, and blessed. May I walk in Your graciousness with a heart to serve.

JACKIE M. JOHNSON

*A spiritual gift is given to each of us
so we can help each other.*

1 CORINTHIANS 12:7 NLT

# Pleasing God

*His pleasure is not in the strength*
*of the horse, nor his delight in the legs*
*of a man; the* LORD *delights in those*
*who fear him, who put their hope*
*in his unfailing love.*

# God's Desire

*Americans* value achievement. We measure our country by its various accomplishments. Scientific discovery, space exploration, technological advancement, and world economic and political power all attest to the hard work and achievement of people building a nation.

As individuals, we measure our days by how much we get done. We take pride in checking items off our to-do lists. We e-mail on our handheld devices while sitting in airports and talk on our phones while driving down the highway in an effort to maximize our time so we can get more accomplished in a day.

God does not place value on our achievements. He does not measure our days by how much we get done. He is not delighted by our efficiency or our excellence. This is pretty hard to believe because our culture places such value on self-reliance, but what pleases Him is our worship of Him. He wants our reverent fear, our wonder and awe at His great power and steadfast love. He desires our dependence. He enjoys our hope when we are looking to Him to meet all our needs.

LEAH SLAWSON

Let us learn to cast
our hearts into God.

BERNARD OF CLAIRVAUX

# Obedience Leads to Joy

*Lord*, Your Word says that if we obey Your commands, we will remain in Your love. I want to serve You out of an obedient, not a rebellious, heart. Just as Jesus submits to You, Father, I choose to submit to You, too. Obedience leads to a blessing. Empower me, encourage me, and give me the will to want to make right decisions, decisions that lead to a better life and greater joy.

JACKIE M. JOHNSON

Meanwhile, the disciples were urging Jesus,
"Rabbi, eat something."
But Jesus replied, "I have a kind of
food you know nothing about."
"Did someone bring him food while we were
gone?" the disciples asked each other.
Then Jesus explained: "My nourishment
comes from doing the will of God, who sent
me, and from finishing his work."

JOHN 4:31–34 NLT

# Spiritual Food

Jesus' purpose on earth was to do God's will. He walked on earth and willingly gave up His life to bring men and women into His heavenly kingdom.

Jesus' disciples were often confused and had difficulty comprehending the meaning behind His words. That's because Jesus emphasized spiritual reality, while they focused on the physical realm. He spoke of establishing a kingdom, and the disciples expected an earthly one. He met physical needs in order to convey spiritual truth.

Like the disciples, we also struggle to focus on spiritual reality. We try to satisfy our souls with physical substitutes. We crave nourishment to alleviate the gnawing hunger in our souls. Attempting to fill the void, we overeat, accumulate possessions, watch TV, or pursue pleasure. Yet we remain unsatisfied.

Try nourishing your soul with spiritual food. Draw close to God. Read His Word. Let Him speak to your heart. Seek to be in the center of God's will. Then you will be nourished, your soul will be satisfied, and your cup will overflow.

JULIE RAYBURN

God wishes to be seen, and He wishes
to be sought, and He wishes to be
expected, and He wishes to be trusted.

JULIAN OF NORWICH

# Blessings for Obedience

Lord, I humbly bow before You and thank You for the power to obey and follow Your ways. It is not easy at times, and I know I could not do it without Your help. Your Word tells us that obedience leads to blessings. I don't want to miss my blessings. I don't want my family or friends—or anyone else—to miss the best in their lives either. So I ask for forgiveness when I have done wrong and strength to make better choices. Help all of us to walk in faithfulness, empowered by Your Holy Spirit.

JACKIE M. JOHNSON

*But what happens when we live God's way?*
*He brings gifts into our lives, much the same way*
*that fruit appears in an orchard—things like*
*affection for others, exuberance about life, serenity.*

GALATIANS 5:22 MSG

Prayer

*And when you are praying, do not use meaningless repetition as the Gentiles do, for they suppose that they will be heard for their many words.*

MATTHEW 6:7 NASB

# Vocalizing a Prayer

*Remember* kneeling beside your bed and praying when you were a kid? Why did it all seem so simple then? We just talked to God like He was really there and kept our requests short and simple.

Then, as you got older, the lengthy and spiritual prayers of the "older saints" became intimidating. So, where's the balance? Reading a little further in this passage from Matthew, at verse 9, Jesus gives us His own example for prayer. If you can remember the acrostic ACTS, you'll have an excellent formula for prayer: Adoration, Confession, Thanksgiving, and Supplication.

As we come before the Lord we first need to honor Him as Creator, Master, Savior, and Lord. Reflect on who He is and praise Him. And because we're human we need to confess and repent of our daily sins. Following this we should be in a mode of thanksgiving. Finally, our prayer requests should be upheld. My usual order for requests is self, family members, and life's pressing issues. Keeping a prayer journal allows for a written record of God's answers.

Your prayers certainly don't have to be elaborate or polished. God does not judge your way with words. He knows your heart. He wants to hear from you.

CAROL L. FITZPATRICK

Prayer is as natural an
expression of faith as
breathing is of life.

JONATHAN EDWARDS

# Strength in God

*Lord*, I know You hear my voice when I pray to You! You are my strength and my shield. When my heart trusts in You, I am overjoyed. You give me courage to meet the challenges of the day. You give me strength to do the tasks You have set before me. You build me up, raise me to the heights, and lead me to places I would never have dreamed were possible. You are the Friend who will never leave me, the Guide who walks before me. With You in my life, I can do anything.

DONNA K. MALTESE

*Very early the next morning,*
*Jesus got up and went to a place*
*where he could be alone and pray.*

MARK 1:35 CEV

# The Priority of Prayer

*Sandy* rubbed the sleep from her eyes and stared at the glowing red numbers on the alarm clock. *Yep. Time to get up.*

She glanced over at her dog, which had crept into her bed after she'd gone to sleep, and envied his simple world. Eat, sleep, fetch the ball, sleep. That was his routine. But hers—*yikes!* Her days were so filled, it was hard to find even a moment's peace. Yesterday nothing had gone right. And today? Who knew? The only thing she did know was that for strength to face the day, she needed to spend some time alone with God. Before her feet touched the floor, she sat up, turned on the light, and grabbed her bedside Bible. In the quiet of the morning, Sandy was determined to spend time with God. Otherwise, how would she ever find her way?

We are to walk as Jesus did. And so we arm ourselves with God's truth and wisdom before our feet hit the floor.

Find your own quiet place where you can be alone. Find a reading plan that will help guide your way through God's Word. And then open up your spirit, heart, and mind to the true reality—life in Christ!

DONNA K. MALTESE

Grant that I may not pray alone with the mouth; help me that I may pray from the depths of my heart.

MARTIN LUTHER

# Rejoice!

*This* is the day that You have made, Lord! I will rejoice and be glad in it! Lord, I feel Your light shining upon me. I feel Your presence all around me. I glory in Your touch! No matter what comes against me today, I know that You will be with me, so there is no reason to be afraid. All I have to do is reach for You and You are here with me. You are so good to me. Thank You, Lord, for Your goodness and Your love.

DONNA K. MALTESE

*Be strong in the Lord and in his mighty power. . . .*
*And pray in the Spirit on all occasions with*
*all kinds of prayers and requests.*

EPHESIANS 6:10, 18 NIV

Rest

*It is a good thing to receive
wealth from God and the
good health to enjoy it.*

ECCLESIASTES 5:19 NLT

# Living a Complete Life

You've probably heard the term *workaholic*, but you may be surprised to find that people really can work themselves to death. The Japanese word *karoshi* is translated literally as "death from overwork," or occupational sudden death. The major medical causes of karoshi deaths are heart attack and stroke due to stress.

It's vital to find a balance in your life between hard work and rest. While you need to earn a living to provide finances to meet your needs, you also want to listen to your physical, mental, emotional, and spiritual needs as well.

God has promised to supply all your needs, but it takes action on your part. Seeking wisdom for your situation and asking God to direct you in the right decisions will help you find a well-balanced life that will produce success, coupled with the health to enjoy it. It may be as simple as realizing a vacation is exactly what you need, instead of working throughout the year and taking your vacation in cash to pay for new bedroom furniture.

Know when to press forward and when to stop and enjoy the life God has given you for His good pleasure—and yours!

SHANNA GREGOR

Rest is not idleness, and to lie sometimes on the grass under the trees on a summer's day, listening to the murmur of water, or watching the clouds float across the sky, is by no means a waste of time.

JOHN LUBBOCK

# The Peace That Brings Life

Lord, I thank You for the peace that restores me mentally, emotionally, and physically. It is the peace that brings wholeness. When my heart is restless, my health suffers. But when I am at peace, You restore my entire body. I can breathe easier, I can relax, and I can smile again because I know everything's going to be all right. You are in control. I thank You that Your peace brings life.

JACKIE M. JOHNSON

*And God said unto Moses,*
*I AM THAT I AM: and he said,*
*Thus shalt thou say unto the children of*
*Israel, I AM hath sent me unto you.*

EXODUS 3:14 KJV

# To Do or To Be?

*Some* women work themselves into a frenzy about the many things they have to do. Others moan about the tasks they are unable to get done, while yet others fret over what they still need to do. The woman who constantly lives with past regrets and future anxieties can be quite unpleasant in the present.

God is not like this. He doesn't regret or fret. Although He existed in eternity past and will be in eternity future, God is neither past nor future. His most revered name is I Am. God is eternally present.

God is. Women are. And women are what they are, where they are, and how they are because God is.

Life is not about doing. Life is about who we are in relationship to who God is.

God's first call to us is to Himself, not to His service. "Come unto me, all ye that labour and are heavy laden, and I will give you rest," Jesus said (Matthew 11:28 KJV).

Be who God wants you to be—rest in Him.

HELEN MIDDLEBROOKE

95

"The LORD bless you and keep you; the LORD make his face shine upon you and be gracious to you; the LORD turn his face toward you and give you peace."

NUMBERS 6:24–26 NIV